# Practical
# Stir-Fry

$p^3$

This is a P³ Book
First published in 2003

P³
Queen Street House
4 Queen Street
Bath BA1 1HE, UK

Copyright © Parragon 2003

All rights reserved. No part of this publication may be reproduced, stored
in a retrieval system, or transmitted, in any form or by any means, electronic,
mechanical, photocopying, recording, or otherwise, without the prior permission
of the copyright holder.

ISBN: 1-40540-941-X

Printed in China

**NOTE**

Cup measurements in this book are for American cups.
This book also uses imperial and metric measurements. Follow the same units
of measurement throughout; do not mix imperial and metric.
All spoon measurements are level: teaspoons are assumed to be 5 ml, and
tablespoons are assumed to be 15 ml. Unless otherwise stated,
milk is assumed to be whole milk, eggs and individual vegetables such as potatoes
are medium, and pepper is freshly ground black pepper.

The nutritional information provided for each recipe is per serving or per person.
Optional ingredients, variations, or serving suggestions have
not been included in the calculations. The times given for each recipe are an approximate
guide only because the preparation times may differ according to the techniques used by
different people and the cooking times may vary as a result of the type of oven used.

Recipes using raw or very lightly cooked eggs should be
avoided by infants, the elderly, pregnant women, convalescents,
and anyone suffering from an illness.

# Contents

# Introduction

One of the quickest, easiest, and most versatile methods of cooking is to stir-fry in a wok. It takes only a few minutes to assemble the ingredients—a selection of vegetables, to which may be added meat, fish, seafood, bean curd, nuts, rice, or noodles. The possibilities are endless for ringing the changes with different oils, seasonings, and sauces, and the result is a colorful, delicious, healthy meal that is as pleasing to the eye as it is to the taste buds.

A wok is a metal pan in the shape of a curved bowl, with one long handle or two looped handles. It comes in a variety of sizes—about 30–35 cm/12–14 inches in diameter is suitable for the average family—and it is worth investing in the best you can. Woks are made from stainless steel, copper, or cast iron. The latter is ideal because it retains heat more efficiently.

Although it is possible to stir-fry in a skillet, the key to successful stir-frying is to move and toss the ingredients constantly as they cook, and this is easier to achieve in the concave shape of a wok. The curved sides let the heat rise, so that the whole wok becomes hot, speeding up the cooking process.

A spatula with a long wooden handle is ideal for stir-frying and removing foods, because the curved edge follows the curve of the wok.

By adding a cooking strainer or shallow wire-meshed basket, the wok may be used for deep-frying, while a steaming trivet and a domed, tight-fitting lid will convert the wok to a very efficient steamer. These extra items may be supplied with the wok when it is purchased.

Before using a new wok, it is essential to season it properly. Use oiled paper towels to wipe the wok both inside and out, then heat it to a high temperature in the oven or on the stove. Remove the wok from the heat, let it cool, then repeat the process several times to create a good, nonstick coating. After the initial seasoning, the wok can simply be wiped clean, or washed in soapy water—but if it is made of cast iron, it is essential to dry it well immediately after washing, to prevent rusting.

## Regional cooking

Although its popularity is now far more wide-ranging, wok cuisine originated in Asia and the Far East. In India, food is cooked in a *karahi*, a large pan that sits over a hole in a brick or earth oven and is used for braising and frying, while in Mongolia, the concave iron griddle used for cooking meat, especially lamb, is similar in shape to a wok.

It was the Chinese, however, who devised stir-frying in a wok. There are regional variations in ingredients throughout this vast country, but fresh vegetables play a very important role. This rapid and efficient method of cooking ensures that vegetables retain their individual flavors, vibrant colors, and crisp texture, as well as preserving their vitamin content. Poultry, lamb, beef, and pork are also cooked in the wok—either stir-fried or steamed—and are combined with sauces and seasonings. Long-grain or short-grain rice is often added or served as an accompaniment, and noodles made from wheat, buckwheat, or rice flours are also widely used.

The Chinese influence has spread to its neighboring countries. Throughout Indonesia, Japan, Thailand, Singapore, and Malaysia the wok is used over wood or charcoal for curries and rice dishes as well as stir-fries, with variations in the meats, fish, spices, and sauces used.

Thai cuisine has enjoyed a huge rise in popularity around the world in recent years. For the people of Thailand, the preparation and eating of good food, beautifully served, is taken very seriously.

The ingredients, locally grown and very fresh, are carefully chosen and skilfully balanced for texture and flavor, combining bitter, salt, sour, hot, and sweet tastes.

The warm seas around Thailand, and the inland waterways, produce a wide variety of fish in abundance, and in all the coastal towns fresh seafood is sold from thatch-roofed beach kiosks—fish cooked with ginger, shrimp cooked with coconut milk and cilantro, or steamed crab. Meat is often combined with seafood such as prawns or crab meat.

Other essentials in Thai cooking are lime, chile, garlic, and lemongrass, as well as seasonings such as soy sauce, rice vinegar, and Thai fish sauce. All of these ingredients are delicious in stir-fries.

## Cooking techniques

Although the wok can be used for steaming and deep-frying, its main use is for stir-frying. In China, where this is the most widely used method of cooking, it is called *Ch'au*, a term that describes cooking a number of ingredients, thinly sliced, in oil. As it cooks, the food is tossed and turned with long bamboo chopsticks.

There are two basic types of stir-frying, known as *Pao* and *Liu*. *Pao*, which could be translated as "explosion," is a method where the food is stirred rapidly in a dry wok over the highest heat for a very short time, about one minute. Foods cooked in this way are often marinated beforehand for flavor and tenderness. *Liu*, on the other hand, could be loosely termed "wet" cooking, and the foods are constantly turned until cooked. Peanut oil or corn oil are usually used for stir-frying. Sesame oil can also be used. It burns easily, and can be drizzled over the finished dish as a seasoning.

Some foods need a slightly longer cooking time than others and, for this reason, stir-frying is often done in stages. This also lets the individual ingredients retain their distinct flavors. As they cook, the foods are removed from the wok, but they are always combined once everything is cooked, and served as a whole dish. It is important not to overfill the wok or the food will steam instead of stir-fry.

In *Liu* cuisine, a mixture of cornstarch and bouillon is added to the wok at the end of cooking, together with sugar, vinegar, and soy sauce, to make a delicious, almost sticky coating sauce.

There is plenty of scope for creativity when choosing ingredients, even for the simplest stir-fry. A combination of onions, carrots, bell peppers (green, red, yellow, and orange), broccoli, and snow peas will provide the basis for a colorful dish. Add bean sprouts at the end of cooking and toss quickly for texture, or try some canned water chestnuts, which add a delicious crunch. A few cashews or almonds, some cubed bean curd or chicken breast, or a handful of shrimp provide protein, and adding pre-cooked rice or noodles will make a more substantial stir-fry. A ready-made sauce, such as oyster or yellow bean, will finish off the dish.

Ginger, garlic, and chiles are marvelous flavorings for stir-fries. Chiles vary widely, from very mild to fiery hot. Red chiles are slightly sweeter and milder than green, and larger chiles also tend to be milder. Crushed dried chilies are useful for seasoning. Thais favor the small red or green "bird-eye" chiles, which are very fiery, and their curries are flavored with ferociously hot chili pastes. Some of the heat can be taken out of a hot chile by removing the seeds, but this must be done very carefully because they can cause a nasty reaction. Cut fresh chiles in half, and scrape out the seeds with the point of a knife. With dried chilies, cut off the end and shake out the seeds. Always wash your hands after handling chiles!

### KEY

 Simplicity level 1–3 (1 easiest, 3 slightly harder)

 Preparation time

 Cooking time

# Ginger & Orange Broccoli

Thinly sliced broccoli florets are lightly stir-fried and served in a delightful ginger and orange sauce.

## NUTRITIONAL INFORMATION

Calories . . . . . . .133   Sugars . . . . . . . . .6g
Protein . . . . . . . . .9g   Fat . . . . . . . . . . .7g
Carbohydrate . . .10g   Saturates . . . . . . .1g

5 mins    10 mins

### SERVES 4

## INGREDIENTS

1 lb 10 oz/750 g broccoli

2 thin slices fresh gingerroot

2 garlic cloves

1 orange

2 tsp cornstarch

1 tbsp light soy sauce

½ tsp sugar

4 tbsp water

2 tbsp vegetable oil

1 Divide the broccoli into small florets. Peel the stems, using a vegetable peeler, and then cut the stems into thin slices, using a sharp knife.

2 Cut the gingerroot into thin sticks and slice the garlic.

3 Peel 2 long strips of rind from the orange and cut into thin strips. Place the strips in a bowl, cover with cold water, and set aside.

4 Squeeze the juice from the orange and mix with the cornstarch, light soy sauce, sugar, and water.

5 Heat the vegetable oil in a wok or large skillet. Add the sliced broccoli stems and stir-fry for 2 minutes.

6 Add the ginger slices, garlic, and broccoli florets and stir-fry for another 3 minutes.

7 Stir the orange and soy sauce sauce mixture into the wok and cook, stirring constantly, until the sauce has thickened and coated the broccoli.

8 Drain the reserved orange rind and stir into the wok. Transfer to a serving dish and serve immediately.

## VARIATION

This dish could be made with cauliflower, if you prefer, or a mixture of cauliflower and broccoli.

# Honey-Fried Spinach

This stir-fry is the perfect accompaniment to bean curd dishes and it is marvelously quick and simple to make.

## NUTRITIONAL INFORMATION

Calories .......146   Sugars .........9g
Protein .........4g   Fat ...........9g
Carbohydrate ...10g   Saturates .......2g

5 mins   15 mins

### SERVES 4

## INGREDIENTS

4 scallions

3 tbsp peanut oil

12 oz/350 g shiitake mushrooms, sliced

2 garlic cloves, crushed

12 oz/350 g baby leaf spinach

2 tbsp dry sherry

2 tbsp honey

1 Using a sharp knife, thickly slice the scallions on the diagonal.

2 Heat the peanut oil in a large preheated wok or in a skillet with a heavy bottom.

3 Add the shiitake mushrooms to the pan and stir-fry for about 5 minutes, or until they have softened.

4 Stir the crushed garlic into the pan. Add the baby leaf spinach and stir-fry for another 2–3 minutes, or until the spinach leaves have just begun to wilt.

5 Combine the dry sherry and honey in a small bowl, stirring until thoroughly mixed. Drizzle the sherry and honey

mixture over the spinach and heat through over low heat, stirring gently to coat the spinach leaves thoroughly in the mixture.

6 Transfer the stir-fry to warm serving dishes, scatter with the sliced scallions, and serve immediately.

### COOK'S TIP

Single-flower honey has a better, more individual flavor than blended honey. Acacia honey is typically Chinese, but you could also try clover, lemon blossom, lime flower, or orange blossom.

# Vegetable Stir-Fry

A range of delicious flavors are captured in this simple recipe, which is ideal if you are in a hurry.

## NUTRITIONAL INFORMATION

| | | | |
|---|---|---|---|
| Calories | .......138 | Sugars | .........5g |
| Protein | .........3g | Fat | ..........12g |
| Carbohydrate | ....5g | Saturates | .......2g |

5 mins    20 mins

### SERVES 4

### I N G R E D I E N T S

3 tbsp vegetable oil

8 pearl onions, halved

1 eggplant, cubed

8 oz/225 g zucchini, sliced

8 oz/225 g open-cap mushrooms, halved

2 garlic cloves, crushed

14 oz/400 g canned chopped tomatoes

2 tbsp sundried tomato paste

2 tbsp soy sauce

1 tsp sesame oil

1 tbsp Chinese rice wine or dry sherry

freshly ground black pepper

fresh basil leaves, to garnish

## COOK'S TIP

Basil has a very strong flavor, which is perfect with vegetables and Chinese flavorings. Instead of using basil simply as a garnish in this dish, try adding a handful of fresh basil leaves to the stir-fry in step 4.

1 Heat the vegetable oil in a large preheated wok or skillet.

2 Add the pearl onions and eggplant to the pan and cook for 5 minutes, or until the vegetables are golden and just beginning to soften.

3 Add the sliced zucchini, mushrooms, garlic, chopped tomatoes, and sundried tomato paste to the pan and cook for about 5 minutes. Reduce the heat and simmer for 10 minutes, or until the vegetables are tender, but not soft.

4 Add the soy sauce, sesame oil, and rice wine or sherry to the wok, bring back to a boil and cook for 1 minute.

5 Season the vegetable stir-fry with freshly ground black pepper and scatter with fresh basil leaves. Serve immediately on warm serving plates.

# Bean Curd Stir-Fry

This is a delicious stir-fry dish, and quick enough to be the perfect choice for a midweek supper after a busy day at work.

## NUTRITIONAL INFORMATION

| | | | |
|---|---|---|---|
| Calories | .......124 | Sugars | .........2g |
| Protein | .........6g | Fat | ...........6g |
| Carbohydrate | ....11g | Saturates | .......1g |

5 mins     25 mins

### SERVES 4

## I N G R E D I E N T S

6 oz/175 g potatoes, cubed

1 tbsp vegetable oil

1 red onion, sliced

8 oz/225 g firm bean curd, diced

2 zucchini, diced

8 canned artichoke hearts, halved

⅔ cup sieved tomatoes

1 tbsp sweet chili sauce

1 tbsp soy sauce

1 tsp superfine sugar

2 tbsp chopped fresh basil

salt and pepper

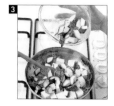

1 Cook the potatoes in a pan of lightly salted boiling water for 10 minutes. Drain thoroughly and then set aside until required.

2 Heat the vegetable oil in a wok or large skillet and stir-fry the red onion for 2 minutes, until softened.

3 Stir in the bean curd and zucchini and stir-fry for 3–4 minutes, until they begin to brown slightly.

4 Add the cooked potatoes to the pan, stirring gently to mix.

5 Stir in the artichoke hearts, sieved tomatoes, sweet chili sauce, soy sauce, sugar, and basil.

6 Season to taste with salt and pepper and cook for another 5 minutes, stirring constantly.

7 Transfer the bean curd and vegetable stir-fry to serving dishes and then serve immediately.

### COOK'S TIP
Canned artichoke hearts should be drained thoroughly and rinsed before use because they often have salt added.

# Mixed Bean Stir-Fry

Any type of canned beans can be used, such as lima beans or black-eye peas, but rinse them under cold water and drain well before use.

## NUTRITIONAL INFORMATION

| | | | |
|---|---|---|---|
| Calories | .......326 | Sugars | ........16g |
| Protein | ........18g | Fat | ...........7g |
| Carbohydrate | ...51g | Saturates | ......1g |

10 mins    10 mins

### SERVES 4

## I N G R E D I E N T S

14 oz/400 g canned red kidney beans

14 oz/400 g canned cannellini beans

6 scallions

7 oz/200 g canned pineapple rings or pieces in natural juice, chopped

2 tbsp pineapple juice

3–4 pieces of preserved ginger

2 tbsp ginger syrup from the jar

thinly pared rind of ½ lime or lemon, cut into thin strips

2 tbsp lime juice or lemon juice

2 tbsp soy sauce

1 tsp cornstarch

1 tbsp sesame oil

4 oz/115 g green beans, cut into 1½-inch/4-cm lengths

8 oz/225 g canned bamboo shoots

salt and pepper

1 Drain the red kidney beans and cannellini beans, rinse under cold water, and drain again very thoroughly.

2 Cut 4 scallions into narrow diagonal slices. Thinly slice the remainder and reserve for garnish.

3 Combine the pineapple and juice, ginger and syrup, lime rind and juice, soy sauce, and cornstarch in a bowl.

4 Heat the oil in the wok, swirling it around until really hot. Add the diagonally sliced scallions and stir-fry for about a minute, then add the green beans. Drain and thinly slice the bamboo shoots, add to the wok, and continue to stir-fry for 2 minutes.

5 Add the pineapple and ginger mixture and bring just to a boil. Add the canned beans and stir until very hot—for about a minute.

6 Season to taste with salt and pepper, sprinkle with the reserved chopped scallions, and serve.

## COOK'S TIP

Beans are an important source of protein for vegetarians. Combine them with rice or other cereals for a really healthy balance.

# Stir-Fried Bean Sprouts

Be sure to use fresh bean sprouts, rather than the canned variety, for this crunchy-textured dish.

## NUTRITIONAL INFORMATION

Calories ........98  Sugars .........2g
Protein .........2g  Fat ...........9g
Carbohydrate ....3g  Saturates .......1g

  5 mins      5 mins

### SERVES 4

## INGREDIENTS

3 cups fresh bean sprouts

2–3 scallions

1 medium red chile (optional)

3 tbsp vegetable oil

½ tsp salt

½ tsp sugar

1 tbsp light soy sauce

a few drops of sesame oil (optional)

1 Rinse the bean sprouts in cold water, discarding any husks or small pieces that float to the top.

2 Drain the bean sprouts well on absorbent paper towels.

3 Using a sharp knife, cut the scallions into short pieces.

4 Thinly shred the red chile, if using, discarding the seeds.

5 Heat the vegetable oil in a preheated wok, swirling the oil around the bottom of the wok until it is really hot.

6 Add the bean sprouts, scallions, and chile (if using) to the wok, and stir-fry the mixture for about 2 minutes.

7 Add the salt, sugar, soy sauce, and sesame oil (if using) to the mixture in the wok, and stir well to blend thoroughly. Serve the bean sprouts immediately, or let cool and serve chilled.

## COOK'S TIP

The red chile gives a bite to this dish—leave the seeds in for an even hotter taste. If you prefer a milder, sweeter flavor, use red bell pepper instead of the chile pepper. Core, seed, and cut into strips in the same way.

# Cantonese Garden Vegetables

This dish tastes as fresh as it looks. Try to get hold of baby vegetables because they look and taste so much better in this dish.

## NUTRITIONAL INFORMATION

| | | |
|---|---|---|
| Calories | . . . . . . .130 | Sugars . . . . . . . . .8g |
| Protein | . . . . . . . . .6g | Fat . . . . . . . . . . .8g |
| Carbohydrate | . . . .8g | Saturates . . . . . . .1g |

5 mins     10 mins

### SERVES 4

## I N G R E D I E N T S

2 tbsp peanut oil

1 tsp Chinese five-spice powder

3 oz/85 g baby carrots, halved

2 celery stalks, sliced

2 baby leeks, sliced

2 oz/55 g snow peas

4 baby zucchini, halved lengthwise

8 baby corn cobs

8 oz/225 g firm marinated bean curd, cubed

4 tbsp fresh orange juice

1 tbsp honey

cooked rice or noodles, to serve

### TO GARNISH

celery leaves

orange rind, cut into strips

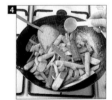

## VARIATION

Lemon juice would be just as delicious as the orange juice in this recipe, but use 3 tablespoons instead of 4 tablespoons.

1 Heat the peanut oil in a preheated wok or large, heavy skillet until almost smoking.

2 Add the Chinese five-spice powder, carrots, celery, leeks, snow peas, zucchini, and corn cobs, and stir-fry for 3–4 minutes.

3 Add the bean curd to the pan and then cook for another 2 minutes, constantly stirring, but gently so that the bean curd does not break up into smaller pieces.

4 Stir the fresh orange juice and honey into the pan, reduce the heat, and cook for 1–2 minutes.

5 Transfer the stir-fry to a serving dish, garnish with celery leaves and orange rind, and serve with rice or noodles.

# Eight Jewel Vegetables

This recipe, as the title suggests, is a colorful mixture of eight vegetables, cooked in a black bean and soy sauce.

| NUTRITIONAL INFORMATION | |
| --- | --- |
| Calories ........110 | Sugars .........3g |
| Protein .........4g | Fat ..........8g |
| Carbohydrate ....7g | Saturates .......1g |

 5 mins    10 mins

### SERVES 4

## INGREDIENTS

2 tbsp peanut oil

6 scallions, sliced

3 garlic cloves, crushed

1 green bell pepper, seeded and diced

1 red bell pepper, seeded and diced

1 fresh red chile, sliced

2 tbsp chopped water chestnuts

1 zucchini, chopped

4½ oz/125 g oyster mushrooms

3 tbsp black bean sauce

2 tsp Chinese rice wine or dry sherry

4 tbsp dark soy sauce

1 tsp dark brown sugar

2 tbsp water

1 tsp sesame oil

1 Pour the peanut oil in a preheated wok or large skillet and heat until it is almost smoking.

2 Lower the heat, then add the scallions and garlic and cook for about 30 seconds.

3 Add the green and red bell peppers, fresh red chile, water chestnuts, and zucchini to the pan and cook for about 2–3 minutes, or until the vegetables are just beginning to soften.

4 Add the oyster mushrooms, black bean sauce, Chinese rice wine or dry sherry, dark soy sauce, dark brown sugar, and water to the pan and cook for another 4 minutes.

5 Sprinkle the stir-fry with sesame oil and serve immediately.

## COOK'S TIP

Eight jewels or treasures form a traditional part of the Chinese New Year celebrations, which start in the last week of the old year. The Kitchen God, an important figure, is sent to give a report to heaven, returning on New Year's Eve in time for the feasting.

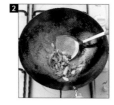

# Lamb with Black Bean Sauce

Red onions add great color to recipes and are perfect in this dish, combining with the colors of the bell peppers.

## NUTRITIONAL INFORMATION

| | |
|---|---|
| Calories .......328 | Sugars .........5g |
| Protein ........26g | Fat ..........20g |
| Carbohydrate ...12g | Saturates .......6g |

10 mins    15 mins

### SERVES 4

### INGREDIENTS

1 lb/450 g lamb neck fillet or boneless leg of lamb

1 egg white, lightly beaten

4 tbsp cornstarch

1 tsp Chinese five-spice powder

3 tbsp sunflower oil

1 red onion

1 red bell pepper, seeded and sliced

1 green bell pepper, seeded and sliced

1 yellow or orange bell pepper, seeded and sliced

5 tbsp black bean sauce

boiled rice or noodles, to serve

1 Using a sharp knife, slice the lamb into very thin strips.

2 Mix together the egg white, cornstarch, and Chinese five-spice powder. Toss the lamb strips in the mixture until evenly coated.

3 Heat the oil in a wok and cook the lamb over high heat for 5 minutes, or until it goes crisp around the edges.

4 Slice the red onion. Add the onion and bell pepper slices to the wok and cook for 5–6 minutes, or until the vegetables just begin to soften.

5 Stir the black bean sauce into the mixture in the wok and heat through.

6 Transfer the lamb and sauce to warm serving plates and serve hot with freshly boiled rice or noodles.

## COOK'S TIP

Take care when cooking the lamb because the cornstarch mixture may cause it to stick to the wok. Move the lamb around the wok constantly while cooking.

# Seafood Stir-Fry

This combination of assorted seafood and tender vegetables flavored with ginger makes an ideal light meal served with thread noodles.

| NUTRITIONAL INFORMATION | |
| --- | --- |
| Calories . . . . . . .226 | Sugars . . . . . . . . .5g |
| Protein . . . . . . . .35g | Fat . . . . . . . . . . .7g |
| Carbohydrate . . . .6g | Saturates . . . . . .1g |

5 mins    15 mins

## SERVES 4

### INGREDIENTS

3½ oz/100 g small, thin asparagus spears, trimmed

1 tbsp sunflower oil

1-inch/2.5-cm piece fresh gingerroot, cut into thin strips

1 leek, shredded

2 carrots, cut into very thin strips

3½ oz/100 g baby corn cobs, cut into fourths lengthwise

2 tbsp light soy sauce

1 tbsp oyster sauce

1 tsp clear honey

1 lb/450 g cooked assorted shellfish, thawed if frozen

freshly cooked egg noodles, to serve

### TO GARNISH

4 cooked jumbo shrimp

small bunch snipped fresh chives

 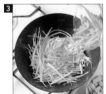 

1 Bring a small pan of water to a boil and then blanch the asparagus for 1–2 minutes.

2 Drain the asparagus, set aside, and keep warm.

3 Heat the oil in a wok or large skillet and cook the ginger, leek, carrots, and corn for about 3 minutes. Do not let the vegetables brown.

4 Add the soy sauce, oyster sauce, and honey to the pan.

5 Add the cooked shellfish and continue to cook, stirring, for 2–3 minutes, until the vegetables are just tender and the shellfish are thoroughly heated through. Add the blanched asparagus and cook for about 2 minutes.

6 To serve, pile the cooked noodles onto 4 warm serving plates and spoon the seafood stir-fry over them.

7 Garnish with the cooked shrimp and snipped fresh chives and serve immediately on warm serving plates.

# Stir-Fried Salmon with Leeks

This salmon is marinated in a deliciously rich, sweet sauce, stir-fried, and served on a bed of crispy leeks.

## NUTRITIONAL INFORMATION

| | | |
|---|---|---|
| Calories .......360 | Sugars .........9g | |
| Protein ........24g | Fat ..........25g | |
| Carbohydrate ....11g | Saturates .......4g | |

35 mins    15 mins

### SERVES 4

## I N G R E D I E N T S

1 lb/450 g salmon fillet, skinned

2 tbsp sweet soy sauce

2 tbsp tomato catsup

1 tsp rice wine vinegar

1 tbsp raw brown sugar

1 garlic clove, crushed

4 tbsp corn oil

1 lb/450 g leeks, thinly shredded

red chiles, finely chopped, to garnish

1 Using a sharp knife, cut the salmon into slices. Place the slices of salmon in a shallow, nonmetallic dish.

2 Mix together the soy sauce, tomato catsup, rice wine vinegar, sugar, and garlic.

3 Pour the mixture over the salmon, toss well, and let marinate for about 30 minutes.

4 Meanwhile, heat 3 tablespoons of the corn oil in a large preheated wok.

5 Add the leeks to the wok and stir-fry over medium-high heat for about 10 minutes, or until the leeks become crispy and tender.

6 Using a slotted spoon, carefully remove the leeks from the wok and transfer to warmed serving plates.

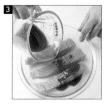

7 Add the remaining oil to the wok. Add the salmon and the marinade to the wok and cook for 2 minutes.

8 Remove the salmon from the wok and spoon over the leeks. Garnish with finely chopped red chiles, and serve immediately.

## VARIATION

You can use a fillet of beef instead of the salmon, if you prefer.

# Stir-Fried Shrimp

The bell peppers in this dish can be replaced by either snow peas or broccoli to maintain the attractive pink-green contrast.

## NUTRITIONAL INFORMATION

| | | | |
|---|---|---|---|
| Calories | ........116 | Sugars | .........1g |
| Protein | ........10g | Fat | ..........6g |
| Carbohydrate | ....4g | Saturates | .......1g |

5 mins     10 mins

### SERVES 4

### INGREDIENTS

6 oz/175 g raw shrimp, peeled

1 tsp salt

¼ tsp egg white

2 tsp cornstarch paste

1¼ cups vegetable oil

1 scallion, cut into short sections

1-inch/2.5-cm piece gingerroot,
   thinly sliced

1 small green bell pepper, cored, seeded,
   and cubed

½ tsp sugar

1 tbsp light soy sauce

1 tsp rice wine or dry sherry

few drops of sesame oil

1 Mix the shrimp with a pinch of the salt, the egg white, and cornstarch paste, until well coated.

2 Heat the oil in a preheated wok and stir-fry the shrimp for 30–40 seconds only. Remove and drain on paper towels.

3 Pour off the oil, leaving about 1 tablespoon in the wok. Add the scallion and ginger to flavor the oil for a few seconds, then add the green bell pepper and stir-fry for about 1 minute.

4 Add the remaining salt and the sugar followed by the shrimp. Continue stirring for another minute or so, then add the soy sauce and wine and blend well. Sprinkle with sesame oil and serve immediately.

### VARIATION

1–2 small green or red hot chiles, sliced, can be added with the green bell pepper to create a spicier dish. You can also leave the chiles unseeded for a very hot dish.

# Tuna & Vegetable Stir-Fry

Fresh tuna is a dark, meaty fish, and is now widely available.
It lends itself perfectly to the rich flavors in this recipe.

| NUTRITIONAL INFORMATION | |
|---|---|
| Calories . . . . . . .245 | Sugars . . . . . . . .11g |
| Protein . . . . . . . .30g | Fat . . . . . . . . . . .7g |
| Carbohydrate . . .14g | Saturates . . . . . . .1g |

🍲 10 mins    🕐 10 mins

### SERVES 4

## I N G R E D I E N T S

3 small carrots

1 onion

6 oz/175 g baby corn cobs

2 tbsp corn oil

6 oz/175 g snow peas

1 lb/ 450 g fresh tuna

2 tbsp fish sauce

1 tbsp palm sugar

finely grated zest and juice of 1 orange

2 tbsp sherry

1 tsp cornstarch

freshly cooked rice or noodles, to serve

1 Using a sharp knife, cut the carrots into thin sticks, slice the onion, and halve the baby corn cobs.

2 Heat the corn oil in a large preheated wok or skillet.

3 Add the carrots, onion, baby corn cobs, and snow peas to the pan and cook for 5 minutes.

4 Using a sharp knife, thinly slice the fresh tuna.

5 Add the tuna slices to the pan and cook for about 2–3 minutes, or until the tuna turns opaque.

6 In a separate bowl, mix together the fish sauce, palm sugar, orange zest and juice, sherry, and cornstarch.

7 Pour the mixture over the tuna and vegetables and cook for 2 minutes, or until the juices thicken. Serve the stir-fry with freshly cooked rice or noodles.

### VARIATION
Try using swordfish steaks instead of the tuna. Swordfish steaks are now widely available and are similar in texture to tuna.

# Squid with Black Bean Sauce

Squid really is marvelous if cooked quickly, as in this recipe; and contrary to popular belief, it is not tough and rubbery unless it is overcooked.

## NUTRITIONAL INFORMATION

| | | |
|---|---|---|
| Calories | ....... 180 | Sugars ......... 2g |
| Protein | ........ 19g | Fat ........... 7g |
| Carbohydrate | ... 10g | Saturates ....... 1g |

5 mins     20 mins

### SERVES 4

## INGREDIENTS

1 lb/450 g squid rings

2 tbsp all-purpose flour

½ tsp salt

1 green bell pepper

2 tbsp peanut oil

1 red onion, sliced

5¾ oz/160 g jar black bean sauce

1 Rinse the squid rings under cold running water and pat thoroughly dry with paper towels.

2 Place the all-purpose flour and salt in a bowl and mix together. Add the squid rings and toss until they are evenly coated. Shake off any excess.

3 Using a sharp knife, seed the bell pepper. Slice the flesh into thin strips.

4 Heat the peanut oil in a large preheated wok or heavy skillet, swirling the oil around the bottom of the pan until it is really hot.

5 Add the sliced green bell pepper strips and red onion to the hot pan and then stir-fry for about 2 minutes, or until all the vegetables are just beginning to soften.

6 Add the squid rings to the pan and then cook for another 5 minutes, or until the squid rings are cooked through and tender. Be careful not to overcook the squid.

7 Add the black bean sauce to the pan and heat through until the cooking juices are just bubbling. Transfer the squid stir-fry to warm serving bowls and serve immediately.

### COOK'S TIP

Serve this recipe with cooked rice or noodles tossed in soy sauce, if desired.

# Fish & Ginger Stir-Fry

This delicious and spicy recipe is a really quick fish dish,
ideal for midweek family meals or light lunches at weekends.

## NUTRITIONAL INFORMATION

Calories . . . . . . .280   Sugars . . . . . . . . .2g
Protein . . . . . . . .31g   Fat . . . . . . . . . .10g
Carbohydrate . . .17g   Saturates . . . . . . .2g

5 mins     15 mins

### SERVES 4

## INGREDIENTS

4 tbsp cornstarch

½ tsp ground ginger

1½ lb/675 g firm white fish fillets, skinned
   and cubed

3 tbsp peanut oil

1-inch/2.5-cm fresh gingerroot, grated

1 leek, thinly sliced

1 tbsp white wine vinegar

2 tbsp Chinese rice wine or dry sherry

3 tbsp dark soy sauce

1 tsp superfine sugar

2 tbsp lemon juice

finely shredded leek, to garnish

1 Mix the cornstarch and ground ginger
in a bowl.

2 Add the cubes of fish, in batches, to
the cornstarch mixture in the bowl,

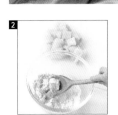  

turning until the fish is thoroughly coated
in the mixture.

3 Heat the peanut oil in a preheated
wok or large, heavy-bottomed skillet,
swirling the oil around the bottom of the
pan until it is really hot.

4 Add the grated fresh ginger and sliced
leek to the pan and then stir-fry for
1 minute.

5 Add the coated fish to the pan and
cook for another 5 minutes, until
browned, stirring to prevent the fish from
sticking to the bottom of the pan.

6 Add the remaining ingredients and
cook over low heat for 3–4 minutes,
until the fish is cooked through.

7 Transfer to a serving dish, garnish with
shredded leek, and serve immediately.

## VARIATION

You can use any firm white fish
that will hold its shape, such
as cod, haddock, or monkfish.

# Scallops in Ginger Sauce

Scallops are both attractive and delicious. Cooked with ginger and orange, this dish is perfect served with plain rice.

## NUTRITIONAL INFORMATION

| | | |
|---|---|---|
| Calories . . . . . . . .216 | Sugars . . . . . . . . .4g | |
| Protein . . . . . . . .30g | Fat . . . . . . . . . . .8g | |
| Carbohydrate . . . .8g | Saturates . . . . . . .1g | |

 5 mins    🕐 10 mins

### SERVES 4

## I N G R E D I E N T S

2 tbsp vegetable oil

1 lb/450 g scallops, cleaned and halved

2 tsp finely chopped fresh gingerroot

3 garlic cloves, crushed

2 leeks, shredded

¾ cup peas

4½ oz/125 g canned bamboo shoots, drained and rinsed

2 tbsp light soy sauce

2 tbsp unsweetened orange juice

1 tsp superfine sugar

strips of orange zest, to garnish

1 Heat the vegetable oil in a preheated wok or large, heavy-bottomed skillet. Add the scallops and then cook for 1–2 minutes. Remove the scallops from the pan with a slotted spoon and keep them warm until required.

2 Add the ginger and garlic to the pan and cook for 30 seconds. Add the leeks and peas and cook, stirring, for another 2 minutes.

3 Add the bamboo shoots and return the scallops to the pan. Stir gently to mix without breaking up the scallops.

4 Stir in the soy sauce, orange juice, and superfine sugar and cook for 1–2 minutes.

5 Transfer the stir-fry to a serving dish, garnish with the orange zest, and serve immediately.

## COOK'S TIP

The edible parts of a scallop are the round white muscle and the orange and white coral or roe. The frilly skirt surrounding the muscle—the gills and mantle—may be used for making shellfish bouillon. All other parts should be discarded.

# Chicken with Vegetables

Coconut adds a creamy texture and delicious flavor to this stir-fry, which is spiked with chopped chile.

## NUTRITIONAL INFORMATION

| | |
|---|---|
| Calories .......330 | Sugars .........4g |
| Protein ........23g | Fat ..........24g |
| Carbohydrate ....6g | Saturates ......10g |

10 mins     10 mins

### SERVES 4

### INGREDIENTS

3 tbsp sesame oil

12 oz/350 g chicken breast, thinly sliced

salt and pepper

8 shallots, sliced

2 garlic cloves, finely chopped

1-inch/2.5-cm piece fresh gingerroot, grated

1 green or red chile, finely chopped

1 red bell pepper, thinly sliced

1 green bell pepper, thinly sliced

3 zucchini, thinly sliced

2 tbsp ground almonds

1 tsp ground cinnamon

1 tbsp oyster sauce

¼ cup creamed coconut, grated

1 Heat the sesame oil in a preheated wok or large skillet.

2 Add the chicken slices to the pan, season with salt and pepper to taste, then stir-fry for about 4 minutes, until the chicken is lightly colored.

3 Add the shallots, garlic, ginger, and chile and stir-fry for 2 minutes.

4 Add the red and green bell peppers, and the zucchini, and cook for about 1 minute.

5 Finally, add the ground almonds, cinnamon, oyster sauce, and coconut. Stir-fry for 1 minute.

6 Transfer to a warm serving dish and serve immediately.

## VARIATION

You can vary the vegetables in this dish according to seasonal availability or whatever you have at hand. Try broccoli florets or baby corn cobs.

# Stir-Fried Ginger Chicken

The oranges add color and piquancy to this refreshing dish, and complement the chicken well.

## NUTRITIONAL INFORMATION

Calories ........289  Sugars ........15g
Protein ........20g  Fat ...........9g
Carbohydrate ...17g  Saturates ......2g

 5 mins      20 mins

### SERVES 4

## I N G R E D I E N T S

2 tbsp sunflower oil

1 onion, sliced

2 carrots, cut into thin sticks

1 garlic clove, crushed

12 oz/350 g boneless skinless chicken breasts

2 tbsp grated fresh gingerroot

1 tsp ground ginger

4 tbsp sweet sherry

1 tbsp tomato paste

1 tbsp raw brown sugar

generous ⅓ cup orange juice

1 tsp cornstarch

1 orange, peeled and segmented

snipped fresh chives, to garnish

1 Heat the oil in a large preheated wok. Add the onion, carrots, and garlic and cook over high heat for 3 minutes, or until the vegetables begin to soften.

2 Slice the chicken into thin strips. Add to the wok with the fresh and ground ginger. Cook for another 10 minutes, or until the chicken is well cooked through and golden in color.

3 Mix together the sherry, tomato paste, sugar, orange juice, and cornstarch in a bowl. Stir the mixture into the wok and heat through, until the mixture bubbles and the juices start to thicken.

4 Add the orange segments and carefully toss to mix.

5 Transfer the stir-fried chicken to warm serving bowls and garnish with snipped fresh chives. Serve immediately.

**COOK'S TIP**

Make sure that you do not continue cooking the dish once the orange segments have been added in step 4, otherwise they will break up.

# Kung Po Chicken

In this recipe, cashews are used but peanuts, walnuts, or almonds can be substituted, if preferred.

## NUTRITIONAL INFORMATION

| | | |
|---|---|---|
| Calories .......294 | Sugars .........3g | |
| Protein ........21g | Fat ..........18g | |
| Carbohydrate ...10g | Saturates .......4g | |

 10 mins    5 mins

### SERVES 4

## I N G R E D I E N T S

9–10½ oz/250–300 g chicken meat, boned and skinned

¼ tsp salt

⅛ egg white

1 tsp cornstarch

2 tsp water

1 medium green bell pepper, cored and seeded

4 tbsp vegetable oil

1 scallion, cut into short sections

a few small slices of gingerroot

4–5 small, dried, red chiles, soaked, seeded, and shredded

2 tbsp yellow bean sauce

1 tsp rice wine or dry sherry

4½ oz/125 g cashews, roasted

a few drops of sesame oil

boiled rice, to serve

1 Cut the chicken into small cubes about the size of sugar lumps. Place the chicken in a small bowl and mix with the salt and egg white. Mix the cornstarch with the water and stir into the chicken mixture.

2 Cut the green bell pepper into cubes or triangles about the same size as the chicken pieces.

3 Heat the oil in a wok, add the chicken and stir-fry for 1 minute. Remove with a slotted spoon and keep warm.

4 Add the scallion, ginger, chiles, and green bell pepper. Stir-fry for 1 minute, then add the chicken mixture with the yellow bean sauce and the wine. Blend well and stir-fry for another minute. Finally, stir in the cashews and sesame oil. Serve hot with boiled rice.

### VARIATION

Any nuts can be used in place of the cashews, if preferred. The important point is the crunchy texture, which is the distinctive feature of this dish.

# Chicken & Black Bean Sauce

This tasty chicken stir-fry is quick and easy to make and is full of fresh flavors and crunchy vegetables.

## NUTRITIONAL INFORMATION

Calories . . . . . . .205   Sugars . . . . . . . . .4g
Protein . . . . . . . .25g   Fat . . . . . . . . . . .9g
Carbohydrate . . . .6g   Saturates . . . . . . .2g

40 mins     10 mins

### SERVES 4

## I N G R E D I E N T S

15 oz/425 g chicken breasts, thinly sliced

pinch of salt

pinch of cornstarch

2 tbsp oil

1 garlic clove, crushed

1 tbsp black bean sauce

1 small red bell pepper, cut into strips

1 small green bell pepper, cut into strips

1 red chile, finely chopped

1 cup sliced mushrooms

1 onion, chopped

6 scallions, chopped

1 tsp cornstarch, blended with
   2 tsp rice wine

freshly cooked noodles, to serve

## S E A S O N I N G

½ tsp salt

½ tsp sugar

3 tbsp chicken bouillon

1 tbsp dark soy sauce

2 tbsp beef bouillon

2 tbsp rice wine

salt and pepper

1 Put the chicken slices in a bowl. Add a pinch of salt and a pinch of cornstarch and cover with water. Let stand for 30 minutes.

2 Heat 1 tablespoon of the oil in a wok or deep-sided skillet and stir-fry the chicken for 4 minutes.

3 Remove the chicken to a warm serving dish and clean the pan.

4 Pour the remaining oil into the pan and add the garlic, black bean sauce, red and green bell peppers, chile, mushrooms, onion, and scallions. Stir-fry for 2 minutes then return the chicken to the pan.

5 Add the seasoning ingredients, cook for 3 minutes, then thicken with a little of the cornstarch blend. Serve with freshly cooked noodles.

# Duck with Leek & Cabbage

Duck is a strongly flavored meat, which benefits from the added citrus peel to counteract this rich taste.

## NUTRITIONAL INFORMATION

Calories .......192    Sugars .........5g
Protein ........26g    Fat ...........7g
Carbohydrate ....6g    Saturates .......2g

🍲 10 mins    🕐 40 mins

### SERVES 4

## INGREDIENTS

4 duck breasts

12 oz/350 g green cabbage

8 oz/225 g leeks, sliced

finely grated zest of 1 orange

6 tbsp oyster sauce

1 tsp sesame seeds, toasted, to serve

1 Heat a large wok and dry-cook the duck breasts, with the skin on, for about 5 minutes on each side (you may need to do this in 2 batches).

2 Remove the wok from the heat, lift out the duck breasts, and transfer them to a clean cutting board.

3 Using a sharp knife, cut the duck breasts into thin slices.

4 Remove all but 1 tablespoon of the fat left in the wok; discard the rest.

5 Using a sharp knife, thinly shred the green cabbage.

6 Reheat the fat in the wok, add the sliced leeks, shredded green cabbage, and grated orange zest and stir-fry for about 5 minutes, or until the vegetables have softened.

7 Return the duck to the wok and heat through for 2–3 minutes.

8 Drizzle the oyster sauce over the mixture in the wok, toss well until all the ingredients are combined, and then heat through.

9 Scatter the stir-fry with toasted sesame seeds, transfer to a warm serving dish, and serve hot.

## VARIATION

Use napa cabbage for a lighter, sweeter flavor instead of the green cabbage, if you prefer.

# Fruity Duck Stir-Fry

The pineapple and plum sauce add a sweet and fruity flavor to this colorful recipe, which blends well with the duck.

## NUTRITIONAL INFORMATION

| | | |
|---|---|---|
| Calories . . . . . . . .241 | Sugars . . . . . . . . .7g | |
| Protein . . . . . . . .26g | Fat . . . . . . . . . . .8g | |
| Carbohydrate . . .16g | Saturates . . . . . . .2g | |

🥟 5 mins    🕐 25 mins

### SERVES 4

## I N G R E D I E N T S

4 duck breasts

1 tsp Chinese five-spice powder

1 tbsp cornstarch

1 tbsp chili oil

8 oz/225 g baby onions, peeled

2 garlic cloves, crushed

1 cup baby corn cobs

1¼ cups canned pineapple chunks, drained

6 scallions, sliced

1 cup bean sprouts

2 tbsp plum sauce

1 Remove any skin from the duck breasts. Cut the duck into thin slices.

2 Mix together the five-spice powder and the cornstarch. Toss the duck in the mixture, until well coated.

3 Heat the oil in a preheated wok. Stir-fry the duck for 10 minutes, or until just beginning to go crisp around the edges. Remove from the wok and set aside.

4 Add the onions and garlic to the wok and stir-fry for 5 minutes, or until softened. Add the baby corn cobs and then stir-fry for another 5 minutes. Add the pineapple, scallions, and bean sprouts and stir-fry for 3–4 minutes. Stir in the plum sauce.

5 Return the cooked duck to the wok and toss until well mixed. Transfer to warm serving dishes and serve hot.

### COOK'S TIP

Buy pineapple chunks in natural juice rather than syrup for a fresher flavor. If you can only obtain pineapple in syrup, rinse it in cold water and drain thoroughly before using.

# Stir-Fried Pork & Cabbage

Rustle up this quick dish in a matter of moments. Assemble all your ingredients first, then everything is ready at hand as you start to stir-fry.

## NUTRITIONAL INFORMATION

Calories . . . . . . .226   Sugars . . . . . . . . .2g
Protein . . . . . . . .21g   Fat . . . . . . . . . .12g
Carbohydrate . . . .4g   Saturates . . . . . . .3g

5 mins      10 mins

### SERVES 4

## INGREDIENTS

13 oz/375 g pork tenderloin

8 scallions, trimmed

½ small white cabbage

½ cucumber

2 tsp finely grated fresh gingerroot

1 tbsp fish sauce or light soy sauce

2 tbsp dry sherry

2 tbsp water

2 tsp cornstarch

1 tbsp chopped fresh mint or cilantro

2 tbsp sesame oil

salt and pepper

### TO GARNISH

sprigs of fresh mint or cilantro

1 chile flower (see Cook's Tip, below)

## COOK'S TIP

To make chile flowers, hold the stem of the chile and cut down its length several times with a sharp knife. Place in a bowl of chilled water and chill so that the "petals" turn out. Remove the chile seeds when the "petals" have opened.

1 Slice the pork very thinly. Shred the scallions and cabbage, and cut the cucumber into matchsticks.

2 In a separate bowl, mix together the ginger, fish sauce or soy sauce, sherry, water, cornstarch, and chopped mint or cilantro, until blended.

3 Heat the sesame oil in a wok and add the pork. Stir-fry briskly over high heat for about 4–5 minutes, until browned.

4 Add the scallions, cabbage, and cucumber and stir-fry for another 2 minutes. Add the cornstarch mixture and continue to stir-fry for 1 minute, until slightly thickened. Season to taste.

5 Transfer the stir-fry to a warmed dish and serve at once, garnished with sprigs of fresh mint or cilantro, and a chile flower.

# Pork Satay Stir-Fry

Satay sauce is easy to make and is one of the best-known and loved sauces in Asian cooking. It is perfect with beef, chicken, or pork.

## NUTRITIONAL INFORMATION

Calories .......506  Sugars ........11g
Protein ........31g  Fat ..........36g
Carbohydrate ...15g  Saturates .......8g

10 mins     15 mins

### SERVES 4

## INGREDIENTS

2 small carrots

2 tbsp sunflower oil

12 oz/350 g pork tenderloin, thinly sliced

1 onion, sliced

2 garlic cloves, crushed

1 yellow bell pepper, seeded and
    sliced

5½ oz/150 g snow peas

2¾ oz/75 g fine asparagus

salted peanuts, chopped, to serve

### SATAY SAUCE

6 tbsp crunchy peanut butter

6 tbsp coconut milk

1 tsp chili flakes

1 garlic clove, crushed

1 tsp tomato paste

1 Using a sharp knife, slice the carrots into thin sticks.

2 Heat the oil in a large, preheated wok. Add the pork, onion, and garlic and stir-fry for 5 minutes, or until the pork is cooked through.

3 Add the carrots, bell pepper, snow peas, and asparagus to the wok, and cook for 5 minutes.

4 To make the satay sauce, place the peanut butter, coconut milk, chili flakes, garlic, and tomato paste in a small pan and heat gently, stirring, until well combined. Be careful not to let the sauce stick to the bottom of the pan.

5 Transfer the stir-fry to warm serving plates. Spoon the satay sauce over the stir-fry and scatter with chopped peanuts. Serve immediately.

## COOK'S TIP

Cook the sauce just before serving because it tends to thicken very quickly and will become very solid if you cook it too far in advance.

# Sesame Lamb Stir-Fry

This is a very simple, but delicious dish, in which lean pieces of lamb are cooked in sugar and soy sauce and then sprinkled with sesame seeds.

## NUTRITIONAL INFORMATION

Calories .......276    Sugars .........4g
Protein ........25g    Fat ..........18g
Carbohydrate ....5g    Saturates .......6g

5 mins        10 mins

### SERVES 4

## INGREDIENTS

1 lb/450 g boneless lean lamb

2 tbsp peanut oil

2 leeks, sliced

1 carrot, cut into matchsticks

2 garlic cloves, crushed

⅓ cup lamb bouillon or vegetable bouillon

2 tsp light brown sugar

1 tbsp dark soy sauce

4½ tsp sesame seeds

1 Using a sharp knife, cut the lamb into thin strips.

2 Pour the peanut oil in a preheated wok or large skillet, and heat until it is really hot.

3 Add the lamb and cook for about 2–3 minutes. Remove the lamb from the wok with a slotted spoon and set aside until required.

4 Add the leeks, carrot, and garlic to the pan and cook in the remaining oil for 1–2 minutes.

5 Use a slotted spoon to remove the vegetables from the wok and set aside.

6 Drain any remaining oil from the pan. Place the lamb bouillon or vegetable bouillon, light brown sugar, and dark soy sauce in the pan and add the lamb. Cook, stirring constantly, for 2–3 minutes.

7 Sprinkle the sesame seeds over the top, turning until the lamb is coated.

8 Spoon the leek, carrot, and garlic mixture onto a warm serving dish and top with the lamb. Serve immediately.

## COOK'S TIP

Be careful not to burn the sugar in the pan when heating and coating the meat, otherwise the flavor of the dish will be spoiled.

# Stir-Fried Lamb with Orange

Oranges and lamb are a great combination because the citrus flavor offsets the fattier, fuller flavor of the lamb.

## NUTRITIONAL INFORMATION

| | |
|---|---|
| Calories . . . . . . .209 | Sugars . . . . . . . . .4g |
| Protein . . . . . . . .25g | Fat . . . . . . . . . .10g |
| Carbohydrate . . . .5g | Saturates . . . . . . .5g |

5 mins        30 mins

### SERVES 4

## I N G R E D I E N T S

1 lb/450 g ground lamb

2 garlic cloves, crushed

1 tsp cumin seeds

1 tsp ground coriander

1 red onion, sliced

finely grated zest and juice of
    1 orange

2 tbsp soy sauce

1 orange, peeled and segmented

salt and pepper

snipped fresh chives, to garnish

1 Heat a wok or large, heavy-bottomed skillet, without adding any oil.

2 Add the ground lamb to the pan. Dry-cook the ground lamb for 5 minutes, or until the meat is evenly browned. Drain away any excess fat from the pan.

3 Add the garlic, cumin seeds, coriander, and red onion to the pan and cook for another 5 minutes.

4 Stir in the finely grated orange zest and orange juice, and the soy sauce, mixing until thoroughly combined. Cover, lower the heat, and let simmer, stirring occasionally, for 15 minutes.

5 Remove the lid, increase the heat and add the orange segments. Stir the orange pieces into the mixture.

6 Season with salt and pepper to taste and then heat through for another 2–3 minutes.

7 Transfer the stir-fry to warm serving plates and garnish with snipped fresh chives. Serve immediately.

### COOK'S TIP

If you wish to serve wine with your meal, try light, dry, white wines and lighter Burgundy-style red wines because they blend well with Asian food.

# Stir-Fried Beef & Vegetables

Beef is perfect for stir-fries because it is very tender and lends itself to quick cooking.

## NUTRITIONAL INFORMATION

Calories . . . . . . . .521   Sugars . . . . . . . . .7g
Protein . . . . . . . .31g   Fat . . . . . . . . . .35g
Carbohydrate . . .18g   Saturates . . . . . . .8g

 10 mins     20 mins

### SERVES 4

## I N G R E D I E N T S

2 tbsp sunflower oil

12 oz/350 g beef fillet, sliced

1 red onion, sliced

6 oz/175 g zucchini

2 carrots, thinly sliced

1 red bell pepper, seeded and sliced

1 small head napa cabbage, shredded

1½ cups bean sprouts

8 oz/225 g canned bamboo shoots, drained

1½ cups cashews, toasted

### S A U C E

3 tbsp medium sherry

3 tbsp light soy sauce

1 tsp ground ginger

1 garlic clove, crushed

1 tsp cornstarch

1 tbsp tomato paste

3 Add the carrots, bell pepper, and zucchini to the pan and cook the mixture for 5 minutes.

4 Toss in the napa cabbage, bean sprouts, and bamboo shoots and heat through for 2–3 minutes, or until the leaves are just beginning to wilt.

5 Scatter the cashews over the stir-fry and toss well to mix.

6 To make the sauce, mix together the sherry, soy sauce, ground ginger, garlic, cornstarch, and tomato paste, until well combined.

7 Pour the sauce over the stir-fry and toss to mix. Let the sauce bubble for 2–3 minutes, or until the juices thicken.

8 Transfer to warm serving dishes and serve at once.

1 Heat the sunflower oil in a preheated wok or large, heavy-bottomed skillet. Add the sliced beef and red onion to the pan and cook for about 4–5 minutes, or until the onion begins to soften and the meat is just browning.

2 Trim the ends from the zucchini and then thinly slice diagonally.